You Might Be Sorry You Read This

You Might Be Sorry You Read This

UNIVERSITY
of **ALBERTA**
PRESS

Michelle Poirier Brown

Published by

University of Alberta Press
1–16 Rutherford Library South
11204 89 Avenue NW
Edmonton, Alberta, Canada T6G 2J4
Amiskwacîwâskahican | Treaty 6 |
Métis Territory
uap.ualberta.ca

LIBRARY AND ARCHIVES CANADA
CATALOGUING IN PUBLICATION

Title: You might be sorry you read this /
    Michelle Poirier Brown.
Names: Poirier Brown, Michelle, author.
Series: Robert Kroetsch series.
Description: Series statement: Robert
    Kroetsch series | Poems.
Identifiers: Canadiana (print) 20210373253 |
    Canadiana (ebook) 20210373261 |
    ISBN 9781772126037 (softcover) |
    ISBN 9781772126136 (PDF)
Classification: LCC PS8631.O379 Y68 2022 |
    DDC C811/.6—dc23

First edition, first printing, 2022.
First printed and bound in Canada by
Houghton Boston Printers, Saskatoon,
Saskatchewan.
Copyediting by Naomi McIlwraith.
Proofreading by Richard Costa.

A volume in the Robert Kroetsch Series.

University of Alberta Press is committed to
protecting our natural environment. As part
of our efforts, this book is printed on Enviro
Paper: it contains 100% post-consumer
recycled fibres and is acid- and chlorine-free.

University of Alberta Press gratefully
acknowledges the support received for its
publishing program from the Government
of Canada, the Canada Council for the Arts,
and the Government of Alberta through the
Alberta Media Fund.

for my father

and the man he found to show me how much he loved me

Contents

one of the functions of poetry
is to make you uncomfortable
    —PÁDRAIG Ó TUAMA, host of *Poetry Unbound*

The Father I Had

His body, bulk,
warm, scrubbed of sweat,
beside me in the pew.
His hand touches
my knee, stills my feet
from swinging. He stands
and I slide off the lip of slick wood,
heft the heavy, red book
onto the pew in front.

He sings tunelessly.
My ear searches the organ tones.
Searches for the voice of Hildegard Calder,
four pews up and across the aisle,
too far to hear her contrary,
alto line.

We were ever worshipful. At home,
the day of rest holy in front of the television
for *Hymn Sing*, shoebox of offering
envelopes on his lap,
ledger on the folding table.
We sang along, the words scrolling,
my ear again hunting the alto.

We shared an April birthday,
tilted the heart-shaped cake toward
the 50mm *Instamatic,* chocolate
because it was his birthday, too.

I like to imagine my daughter's fingertips
on the trick he'd play with his Adam's apple.
That, and stealing noses.

On my night table I keep a photograph,
my father wader-deep in the Red River
dressed for a gentleman's sport,
mouth ajar with intent.

God Was a Baby

It was Christmas Eve,
the Christmas Eve astronauts read from *Genesis*
as they circled the moon,
and the world was agape,
their eyes upward,
everything exactly as it was yesterday,
but the axis of knowledge tilted.

We walked in the street,
the star-sprinkled hard-packed tracks
no less sparkled
than the fresh drifts brimming the sidewalks.

I slid my boots along the wide ridges,
imagined pirouettes, blades
parting the slick surface,
my pleated plaid skirt
a glimmering sheathe
beneath scarf- and mitten-stuffed coat.

God was a baby,
a marvel circled the moon,
the world made of diamonds.

A Child's *Book of Holy Services*

Wooden Scrabble racks make good pews.
Chess-piece pawns await the bride,
the billow of her Kleenex veil fixed to her coronet with elastic.
Horses as groomsmen, slender bishops as maids,
the cross-crowned king as priest.
The game falters at the same juncture every time.

What to do about a groom?
A father?

The child playing here is a girl.

A plastic doll,
the kind with flutter-back blue eyes,
their long, black lashes making up for plastic-formed hair,
receives a baptismal blessing
in the bathroom sink.
The dolly might be the kind that pees when you give it *a bottle*,
or the kind that comes with two bottles,
grey milk and iridescent orange juice,
crisp, clear plastic with pink nipples,
dispensing liquid that disappears without a drop.
Either way,
it is in the name of the father,
the son,
and the holy ghost.

Septuagesima. Graduals.

Barbie doll mothers
have infants that died.
Their stiff arms empty,
they take to their beds,
while priest
and non-existent husband
bury the bit of air
with a spoon.

Her Breath on My Face

Marie Louise Antonia Vigoureux was three years old when her mother died, and she was taken into the charge of the Sisters of Charity, or Grey Nuns, at the orphanage in St. Boniface. From toddlerhood until she was an adult woman, our grandmother lived in the protective world of the convent, a building that stands to this day, treasured as the first oak building in Western Canada. Louis Riel was schooled there, as were hundreds of children, some of them French Canadian, many of them, like my grandmother, Métis.

She was not raised by a mother, a child finding her place among siblings. She slept in a dorm with other girls, spent time on her knees, both in prayer and washing floors, and found her place in a world ordered by the habits of nuns, something she mentioned as often as a veteran might mention the war.

My grandmother's time within the sisterhood was so integral to her definition of self that it became part of my own identity, so much so that when asked to introduce myself by giving my name, where I was from, and, say, something that made me uncommon, my answer was almost inevitably, "My name is Michelle and my grandmother was a nun."

I said this because she said this. Everything about her she attributed either to being raised by the nuns—or to *being* a nun.

The nuns were the reason she was fluent in French and English and could read and write so well in both languages that she was sometimes asked to translate letters and legal documents.

She followed the news closely and read nightly until 4:00 AM. She was drawn to books on politics, history and religion, and enjoyed especially the novels *Exodus* and *The Shoes of the Fisherman*. She made up for the late nights by sleeping until noon.

She read *Mein Kampf* and cheered for dictators of all kinds. She made a point of buying South African wine during apartheid and prided herself for leading a band of scab steel workers through picket lines at the rolling mill, brandishing her way with a walking stick. She read *Time Magazine* every week, passing it on to my father underlined and bristling with marginalia about Khrushchev or the Pope. *Fools!!!! Nonsense! Ha! Fidel!!!*

I expect her convent childhood shaped my grandmother's personality as well as her interests. Frances, as she was known after her noviciate, was outspoken and irascible. In her outrage, often at my mother, she would pull the telephone from the wall and throw it into the garden. She was absolute about people, either showing them endless kindness, doing baskets of mending for them, giving them food—or you were dead to her.

I remember long summer days beside her in the grape arbour, where she smoked through the day playing Scrabble with anyone who came by, her laugh harsh and loud, her hand warm on my cheek as she lowered her whiskered face and whispered, *beautiful.*

Other Side of the Glass

The television fascinated me.
Where did Popeye come from?
If I cut the wire that went from the TV set to the wall,
could I catch Swee'Pea and Olive Oyl before they
got away?
Play with them for real.

The mirror, too, fascinated me.
Especially the room behind the glass above the couch.
My cheek pressed flat,
I tried to see
if the me who lived there had a playmate.

I came to understand *off* and *on*.
Came to understand
there was no other room.
I came to see
the moustache on my upper lip the kids I babysat pointed at.
My stick-out, greasy hair.
The zits that sprouted

and sprouted.

The easier image
after a perm and a shag cut. The Pill
cleared up the zits.
The invention of the curling iron.
Tools that unlocked *attractive*.

Except, not always.

Coming into the bathroom,
a glance in the mirror,
a wince.
You are having an ugly day.
You look like an Indian.

Effect on Her Throat

If you were first afraid when you were very little,
say four, and have been given no reason to stop,
then fear is your default
—lightning strike, a certain result of the
      perfect conditions;
            a ratchet tightening
               her spine,
               through her gut,
               piercing her right eye,

               closing her heart as tight.

The House on Strathnaver Avenue

Ambition

I could pass an hour or more on a summer afternoon practicing the bouncing ball game *One Two Three Alairy* on the driveway. The basic routine for the four-line nonsense poem involved four bounces a line, the end of each line complicated by swinging a leg between hand and ball on the last bounce. If I made it through the poem with my right hand, I'd repeat the routine on the left. With a successful performance on the left, I allowed myself to proceed to the next, more difficult execution: clapping my hands between each bounce, clapping behind me, over my head, beneath my leg, jumping both legs over the ball. Sometimes I would demand of myself a flawless routine, starting again at the very beginning if I hit the ball with my leg or failed to catch it.

Disillusionment

My father worked in the sewers of a steel mill and my mother asked for our new house to include a separate room for him to shower in when he got home. In addition to the shower, the room had a toilet, simple sink, and mirrored medicine cabinet. The cabinet had little in it. A toothbrush for dentures, some toothpaste, a safety razor, shaving soap, and a bottle of Gripe Water my older sister had brought home from a babysitting job with the recommendation it was useful for curing hiccups. I don't recall it ever working. During one episode of hiccups, I concentrated on just how much I disliked the taste of Gripe Water on the theory my aversion to taking a dose could motivate a breath held long enough to defeat the malady.

Independence

The first meal I made for myself was lunch: a lettuce sandwich. White bread. Mayonnaise. Iceberg lettuce. And a glass of milk.

Intimacy

"Don't you think I know none of you like me?"

It seems unjust that this is the only line I can remember from a fight I had with my sister in the middle of an afternoon. It would have been either July or August, the months she was home from boarding school. I stood at one end of the sofa, the end her feet pointed towards. She had been propped against a pillow, reading, but by the time she cried out this truth, she was lying on her side and sobbing.

Satisfaction

My parents took in boarders, a series of female first grade teachers who lived in a main floor bedroom, and ate meals at the same time as family, and Selkirk Steeler hockey players who slept in the basement and didn't.

Once, my parents were away for a week and I was left in the care of the teacher. I do not remember why they were away, only that we wanted the house to look beautiful on their return. I brushed the entire wall-to-wall carpet in the living room with a palm-sized clothes brush. It looked perfect. It showed every footstep.

Play

One year, there wasn't enough money for a Christmas tree. Santa left the presents lined along the living room wall. I received an Ookpik, a toy replica of the fluffy, arctic owl in the comic strip *Ookpik Was Here*. Its orange felt beak reminded me of a carrot. I dutifully slept with it.

Denial

I stood at the top of the steps in our bare and empty garage and read from my mother's bedside book of daily devotionals as though they were sermons and the rake and the snow shovel congregants. The floor was cement, the acoustics excellent.

I wanted to be a preacher. With solemnity, I confessed my dream to my father. My idea pleased him. I could tell it made sense to him. It was the one time I landed on a spot on the pretend-the-future game board that seemed to make him proud. I heard it as a note in his voice when he said, "I think we should tell Pastor Kornfeld." Heard it again, Sunday morning, at the door to the church, shaking hands with the minister, "Pastor Kornfeld, Michelle has something to tell you." Proud. Pleased with me.

This is it, I thought. This is how good things begin. This is how you start to shape your life. You begin when you are 10. You start your studies when you are 10. Then you can make your dream come true.

Or not.

Pastor Kornfeld's face transformed before my uplifted one.

"You couldn't possibly become a minister. That would be heresy. You're a girl."

Telling

I drew courage from the silence, the absence of laughter. My mother was still at the dining room table. The teacher and my father had gone to bed, no evidence of the supply of construction paper circles they'd all been creating for a classroom project left in sight. My mother worked alone, papers and envelopes in stacks before her. The kitchen behind her was in darkness, the light above the table the only one on. I stood at the end of the hall, next to the built-in mahogany china cabinet, wearing a filmy, layered nylon nighty with lace straps and bare feet. I held my elbows for warmth.

My mother neither got up nor called me to her. When I was finished, she said simply, "Okay, now you've told me. Go back to bed."

Defeat

My brother slept in what had been intended to be a sewing room. It was a doorless space at the far end of our long house, on the other side of the doors to the garage and the back yard, on the other side of my father's shower room. The closet in this room was designed for storing winter clothes. It was lined with cedar and airless. I hid there once in a game of hide and seek. The seeker tattled and my triumph was marred by rebuke. I was never to hide there again.

Performance

After watching gymnasts on television in the basement family room, I set two wooden chairs facing each other, stripped to my tights and undershirt, and leapt over them. I made it three times. Tired, I caught my foot on the fourth jump and hit my head on the cement floor. My father called my bruise a beauty of a goose egg.

Boundaries

My brother thought it would be helpful to use lubricant. The first product he tried was Vicks VapoRub. Although he kept it on his windowsill, I asked him the next time not to use it.

Aspiration

The bedroom closets had wooden folding doors. The teacher kept a carton of cigarettes in blue packages on the right corner of the shelf and often left an open pack on her dresser.

In the evening, the teacher and my mother would work together at the dining room table, my mother preparing for the kindergarten class she taught, the teacher marking awkward printing guided by solid and dotted lines. My father was often with them, making cigarettes by filling filtered paper tubes with tobacco with a hand-operated machine. They talked and joked together as they worked.

I began with the open pack and wasn't accused until I'd taken from the closet.

Determination

When the hair on my legs grew dark, I shaved during a bath using the blade in my mother's sewing kit, holding it by the edge covered with electrical tape.

Mothers Who Know

We talk about the children. The girls. The boys. The uncles. The neighbours. The fathers. The sons. The boyfriends. The brothers.

We do not talk about the fathers who don't, but find out.

And we do not talk about the mothers.

The mothers who know.

And are silent.

And those who know

and instruct their daughters to comply.

Not because it has anything to do with power. But because it is her role.

Because it is what sisters of brothers are expected to do.

And that no, she, your mother, does not intend to intervene.

The time will come when you will lie on your bed, knowing. She never came.

She left.

The Thing about Snow

There are two things
      you need to know.
The first thing is helpful,

      when the inevitable happens.

      Childhood can wake at any time.

Twelve years old,
outside, Manitoba,
    January,
      barefoot, summer weight
      pants
      short sleeved shirt.
Snow in Selkirk
      halfway to the windows.
28 below Centigrade
(close to 20 below Fahrenheit)
At that temperature,
      exposed skin freezes
      after 30 minutes,
      faster
      if in contact with water.

My older brother.
    Dangerous,
nineteen,
    home
      after going AWOL

from
the U.S.
Marines.
Run-ins with police,
small scale crimes
(purse snatching).
He'd gone to the U.S.
to start over.

We had an argument.
Could someone
reasonably expect directions
to a colander
when they'd asked
for a strainer?

My brother.
Door to my bedroom.
Raised voice.
Flippant.
Ask for the colander
if that's what you want.

He leaves.
Returns
with a bar-b-q fork.

His girlfriend.
Screams.
Holds him back.

Time enough
open
window
jump.

Snow filled our yard.
The closest refuge—
the parsonage a block and a half
away.

In winter,
sidewalks, roadways,
a thick layer of packed snow.
Sanded intersections,
slick sidewalks.
My feet bare.

The minister's house,
Christmas
choir parties.
Cookies.

My brother.

In two years,
incarcerated
bike gang
murder in Edmonton.

The parsonage.
No answer.

The back doorstep.
Wait.

A woman next door.
A wooden chair, just
inside the back door.
    I turn my head,
       see her
  in the kitchen.
    She uses the phone
on the kitchen wall,
says nothing to me.

Helpful to know this:
    the trauma
    lives in my body
    still.
I am susceptible
    to shock.
  I tremble,
    sometimes quite intensely,
just talking about sensitive
  subjects.
    If aggression,
    outright shock.
I feel faint.
    My teeth chatter.
    Loudly.

Sometime later,
my father came
to take me home.

My mother,
  furious.
  Instigator.

Sent me
to my room.

Any other details
forgotten.

The information about snow
practical,
necessary
to know.
The thing,

in other words,
that I might need
to tell you.

Here's the thing.
The snow is helpful.
The next
essential.

My brother
had sex with me
from the time
I
was
six
years
old
until just before
my first period.

Even more essential—
my mother knew
did nothing
to intervene.

These are things you need to know
before I can get close
enough for
friends.

If the secret
gets out afterward,

at a sleepover party,
say,

I may lose you
as a friend.

Childhood experience tells me,
you might no longer
be allowed.

Photograph

You are a 15-year-old girl.

Four hours in a car with a family you do not know very well and whose house you will be sleeping at.

The purpose of your trip is a destination. A destination with high concrete walls topped by barbed wire and watched over by armed sentries.

You will pass through many locked doors.

To sit across the table from a man who had sex with you when you were six years old.

And for many years afterward.

You will go alone.

Be a good Christian.

That night you will have dinner with this family and they will take a photograph of you holding a large blue balloon, a balloon so large it fills your lap as you sit cross-legged on the floor, your arms draped around it, your cheek against it, your hair to your shoulders and in ringlets.

You like the pants you're wearing.

Under the Covers

My father was cursed with a grim skin disease that infected his sweat glands one by one. The only treatment was to remove each gland surgically.

At first, the operations were performed in a rural hospital two and a half hours from home. My father would be away a week to ten days, and come home with a fresh scar on his face or neck, to a meal of steak and mushrooms — a rare treat. My parents hardly ever hugged or kissed, so a special meal was how my mother showed affection. Even today, the smell of mushrooms frying means to me a loved one is home.

My father seemed untroubled by his scars. He used to say they were good for business, because people never forgot his face. But in time, the surgeries became more drastic. The major glands under his arms became infected, and he was referred to a plastic surgeon in Winnipeg, who deeply excavated the problem area and repaired the damage with skin grafts from my father's thighs. The underarms were done one at a time, three months apart. After each, the affected arm was strapped to a bar above my father's bed for six weeks, until the graft had taken. Later, physical therapy was required to rebuild the arm muscles that had withered from lack of use.

His case was a medical novelty. When my sister, a doctor, married a med school colleague, himself a physician's son, my father was the centre of attention at the wedding. He thought nothing of stripping to the waist so the enormous scars under his arms could be poked and admired by doctors in tuxedos and chiffon.

Over the years, my father had additional surgery on his back and chest. Then, when I was in college, infection erupted in the sweat glands of his groin. I went to visit him a few days after his surgery. His lower body was covered by a cage to keep his blankets from touching him there. As I rested my hands on his bedrails, my mother offered to go get coffee.

"Wait," he said to her in a soft voice. "I looked when they changed the dressings today; I'll understand if you never want me again."

My mother blinked back tears and pressed her lips together. "Never mind that," she said, and left the room.

The Girls I Grew Up with Are Everywhere

The curve of a shoulder
slung along the back of a Cineplex Odeon seat.
The back of a head.
Ruth-L's straight brown mane,
caught behind what can only be her small ear.
She has taken to wearing exclusively
textured clothes, wide-wale corduroy,
soft flannel plaid shirts, pilled with evidence
of washings and dryings and savoured,
repeated wearings.

Ruth turns to laugh with her companion.
She wears a stranger's face, pitted
by the scars of an acned adolescence,
her teeth grown crooked
and mottled. My greeting,
warmed by a decade,
dries in my mouth.

Denise appears most often at crosswalks
and in expensive restaurants.
First her fresh smile and haircut, and second
the Toronto trolley car
bearing down on her, one bike wheel
caught in the tracks.
On her way to her first job interview
since her divorce.

Jil I see in bank lineups,
at drug store counters,
in the audience of concerts
aired on PBS. A few years back,

I called her in Vancouver and we met
for dinner at a Greek restaurant.
I talked about a recent affair,
some "teaching" I was into,
and was probably too impressed
by the male belly dancer's abilities.

She's moved
without sending me a forwarding address.

These women
haunt the corners of my eyes,
and others, like them,
voices behind me at bus stops,
recognizable scents in hotel lobbies.
They smoke cigarettes during intermissions,
even though they probably quit
years ago.
They travel with me to remote islands,
show up at international airports,
and do laundry in unlikely places.

Their laughter sticks
to the bottom of my shoes
like tape.

Short Change

Leaving the Open Space on a Saturday night,
Elizabeth's lament
she hasn't change for the bus
inspires me to dig into my pocketful
of quarters,
brought in case
I couldn't resist a glass of wine.

Here, I say.
Let me buy you a ride home.

Elizabeth protests, knows well
the repurposed jar mentally labelled
Laundry Reserve.

Half-convinced by my off-hand assurance
What the hell, you only live once,
she resignedly
holds out her hand.

Yes, I suppose it's true—you can get your undies
clean if you wash them in a basin but
you can't ride
home in a tub.

Open Space is a non-profit artist-run centre founded in 1972 in Victoria, BC.

After the Test

I order O'Donal's *Light Start*
because it comes with pancakes that taste
the way my mother's would have
had she loved me.

I want only to be left
to cry and sleep,
sit on my brilliant new sofa,
passing time, being pregnant.

The plate comes with a fried egg when
I'd ordered poached.

I don't say anything.

Decide not to waste
the egg.

Walk on the Left-Hand Side

Because you want to see what is coming at you.
Because the ditch on that side is dry.
Because the neighbours will think better of you.
Because that's where you stashed the answers.
Because you see better out of your right eye.
Because you never know.
Because you want to be well lit.
Because you're hoping to pass as somebody else.
Because of the dog who growls at you through the fence.
Because the sun shines warmer there.
Because you're hoping he'll see you.
Because of the book store window.
Because of the wind.
Because lilacs are in bloom.
Because it's in the directions.
Because that was the side you walked on then.

5:53 PM

shouldn't have begun

shouldn't have ended

will never be the same

will never come back   will never matter to anyone but me

shouldn't have shouted

shouldn't have named it

that time I took and didn't pay

knew I couldn't pay enough

shouldn't have called

calling was the only thing to do

shouldn't have answered

the moment the letter dropped through the slot, I knew

shouldn't have bought it

shouldn't have accepted

that moment   then

shouldn'ts   regrets

shouldn't have sent roses

shouldn't have stayed home

shouldn't have gone

the moment of agreeing   the moment past rest

shouldn't have expected
gone on
trusted
opened

    doubted
        laughed
                knew the moment had passed
            the moment I knew it would rain

    knew I shouldn't have spoken
shouldn't have been late
            shouldn't have waited

                    The moment I knew
                    the water was deep.

A Perspective on Women

There is something you learned that I didn't,
         as indelible and necessary as the silken dust of a grey moth.

Male birds do tricks with their syrinx, paths of light slant
                                    through the trees.

I have come to sit. To contemplate my perspective on women.

A perspective as likely to contain *warnings, regrets, promises...*
                              and dreams as anything else.

I consider the fir trees on the far side of the baseball diamond,
         their lithe forms. Their skirts, their fingernails.

Yes, there is something they learned that I didn't.

I have chosen a set of sturdy, weathered, bench-style bleachers,
                              five tiers high, ten seats wide.

The chainlink fence snaps into focus. The distance to the now
                              invisible trees.

A crack in the woods behind me.

Dusk. They won't know where to look.

Collard Greens

If I gave my mother
a fresh stalk of collard greens,
the outreach of their succulent leaves
smooth and translucent as a baby's brow,
she would laugh and say,
What do you want me to do with that?
followed by,
I don't know.

Not, *I don't want to.*
Not, *I don't like brassicas.*
Just, *I don't know.*

No one imagines you a criminal
when you appear incapable of anything.

If my mother gave me
a fresh stalk of collard greens,
I would fold into a kitchen chair,
my elbows on the table,
and feel the things that come to mind
when I imagine prayer.

Lasts

1

After twenty-six years of psychotherapy:
This was as good as I'd get.

2

I intended it to be my last marriage.
People talk of lists, and I suppose
my two criteria comprised a list.
But I did keep it to two.

I would be loved.

He would have his own money.

3

The last *krumkake*.
The last notch in the belt.
The last of the tampons.
The last tailored shirt.
The last Ativan.
The last thing I said to my mother.

4

The last time
I had sex
for money.

5

Halfway down the stairs,
it stopped me:
I need to see my father.

I borrowed my lover's car,
drove the six hours
from Regina to Selkirk,
parked outside the tackle shop.
He was out,
making the round of fishing spots.
Flies, wrigglers, sodas, chips.

He saw the plate in the lot,
came through the door
swinging his face
to find me.

I'm Allowed to Have Whatever Kind of Father I Want

Dad?

Remember that time you said you'd been looking a long time for a way to tell me how much you loved me?

It worked. I feel loved.

What difference? Well.

So before...
well,

before was a lot like having an inaudible fire alarm go off and yank you, like a dog whistle you can't hear but sets you off all the same.

It's quieter now.

I agree. I'm probably less likely to have a heart attack.

No. All the time. I first figured it out when I went to this yoga studio that offered a free meditation class. You count to 10. And so, during the conversation over tea afterwards part, I decided to mention that when I counted, I was shouting. In my head. And the teacher looked at me and he said, I think that's uncommon.

That's when I learned about the fire bell. It was ringing. All the time.

No, no, much better. Much.

I know. It's my first true belly.

No. Really. It's a comfortable life. More than I expected.
It's been odd, actually. I didn't know how to imagine it.

Yes, exciting. I want to write about the steel mill but it's completely changed. And, of course, they're suspicious as hell. It would be easier to get inside the Vatican. It's computerized.

No, really. I'd love to see it.

It's good, it's good. Mostly, so far, about Grandma. Her fence. The time she tore the phone off the wall and threw it into the garden.

No, I'm saving the story about the barium enema.

I know. That and her wedding night.

Dad. I'm good. You can be both dead and happy.

Yes, you chose him well. I am loved.

You're right. It's pure. It is pure.

Intimacy

| after listening to Elena Ferrante in translation

She whispers to me about the time
        she pulled a knife in the school yard,
the man she slept with to have his friends,
the tip she stole from the next table.

Who would tell you these things to your face?

Would I tell you
        I want to catch your necklace,
trace my finger from your clavicle
        to your breast,
feel the chain hurt you
        just the way I want it to?

Who would admit
        not loving a child,
            infections,
      what you've done for money,
          or a ride?

These words on the page slice a line
        that beads with blood.

        Lick here.

On the Porch

1
January.
Night.
The children in their beds.
She sits next to her husband,
and he explains they'll all go camping,
she and the children with him,
a family outing they've never before pulled off
but that he thinks they'd all enjoy
with his lover.

2
In law school, she took up smoking.
If you smoked, you were in the smokers' study group.
When she needs to, she still lights up.
Wants a friend, the calm the smoke unlocks.
On the step at night, cordless phone.

3
Her lover writes from his bike trip to Croatia.
He goes in the lane to steal wifi.
Not everything sent arrives.
She writes, *take the temperature of stones.*
He answers with a photo: sun slants in a country room.
Then a poem with a train in descent,
gaining on the sea, the air in the car
aglint with spring light.
She leans on her warm clapboard and answers,
the trees in bloom along the street

their leaf and pink the stuff
of ladies' dresses.

4

She can trace her history in its ornaments:
the leaded glass, exactly as desired,
obtained in a trade for a 1974 Volvo the children called
the green rocket ship. It felt magnificent,
following as it did
the blue Datsun, with its piece of board
in the rusted trunk, so small objects didn't fall
into the gas tank.

But that was cars ago.

The glass, its grey and clear
        a perfect petalled *fleur*,
still satisfies. Below,
the long-black lion, iron circle through his jaw,
glows gold against the fresh black door.

From here, she hears the world:
the neighbour shovelling gravel, a helicopter over the harbour.
A wet and throaty *I don't want to*
down the street.

She gets a broom, knocks the feeder
her husband put up so she could have chickadees.
Waits for *silly baby*, the juvenile finch
who fell asleep, head against the cup.

At Times, My Teeth Chatter

I am on the sofa in the living room. I've taken the heavy chenille throw from the back of the sofa to see if I can warm my feet.

It is 22 degrees in the house, the default temperature. My hands feel cold to the touch. My feet, because I go sock-less, feel even colder.

Feeling cold is memory, body, identity. Partly it has to do with growing up on the prairies. Growing up on the prairies, you learn how to breathe safely outdoors, how to keep the wind from freezing your cheeks when you're walking. The cold defines the parameters of your experience. I have made love in a snowbank. And I have seen a man's feet as frozen as blocks of ice.

He and his buddy had been heading home on snowmobiles. His buddy had been in the lead. They hit a body of water and the ice was soft. This man, the man sitting in the backseat of my boyfriend's car, this man had jumped off his snowmobile just in time. He watched his machine go below the water, but he'd had enough warning and he was able to get flat on the ice before he went in.

His feet were wet, maybe even his legs. He walked away from the hole in the ice across the field, to the highway. We saw him at the side of the road waving his arms.

My boyfriend flagged down another car and told them to get help. It was 1974.

We turned the heat up in the car and helped the guy get his boots off. I held his feet in my hands, not knowing if that was the right thing to do. I wondered what they would do for his pain. His feet smelled bad. I think the man also smelled of alcohol, although I can't be sure. I remember how incomplete things felt when the man got out to get into the ambulance. I wanted to wash my hands but we were miles from even a gas station.

To grow up on the prairies is to understand every season has its tragedies. The tragedies of winter are piercing, their setting stark and beautiful.

In a sense, the cold of a Manitoba winter owns me. It lives in me, its power sometimes sleeping, but never absent. It can wake anytime the conditions are just right.

In an intimate conversation with a friend, the kind of conversation that touches on private hopes and longings, or explores a mystery in a relationship with another friend, or family member, or a lover, or that surfaces some unsettling disquiet that has been lying hidden, a psychic discomfort that can keep one from knowing what to do next, or makes a simple thing seem hard.

In such conversations, with a spouse, or a daughter, or even a close colleague, I will begin to tremble, to shiver. Sometimes, only I can detect the tremors, other times they are more obvious. My cup will shake visibly as I raise my tea to my lips, or a paper will flutter as I lay it down on a table.

These tremblings started in Grade 12. I was in my third year of boarding school at the Lutheran Collegiate Bible Institute. My room was on the third floor, the last room on the left side of the hall, past the stairs to the attic. I slept in the top bunk. It was a disruptive night. My roommate went for help. She woke the Dean of Girls, brought her from her apartment on the second floor. I had woken from a dream and at the same time felt I could not wake myself. My body felt rigid, as if I was hanging onto something with great effort, as if I was fighting to wake up but fighting also to hang on to sleep.

The Dean of Girls stayed at my side, but also sent for a girl I was asking for. We were not close, this girl and I, but we had been together at school for nearly three years and I had always felt she was steady and kind. Somehow I thought if I could have her presence in the room I could calm myself. She came for a time and then returned to her bed.

Someone went to rouse the school principal and he came from his home to survey the crisis. The drama carried on for quite some time. By the early hours of the morning, my mind felt calmer and I was able to give in to exhaustion and relax the grip I was keeping on consciousness.

The whole experience was humiliating. I felt my behaviour was bizarre and did not want to leave my room the next day. I felt I could not look in the face of any of the other students at the school. When I finally emerged to go to the toilet down the hall, in pain for holding back for so long, I was crushed to see a student sitting in the window seat outside my door.

I slept one more night at the school. The next day, the dean drove me, and the trunk and suitcases that held all my belongings, to the train station in Saskatoon, an hour-long car trip.

I sat silently in the passenger seat, a bag lunch on my lap. I ate the lunch in the train station, the first food I'd had since my nighttime ordeal. I did not say goodbye to anyone. I just wanted to disappear.

I trembled a lot after that night and for a short while received psychiatric care at the hospital in my home town, Selkirk, Manitoba.

I was given a prescription to take to relieve the shivering if it went on too long or became socially awkward.

Then the doctors of the province went on strike. I had been in psychiatric care long enough for an initial assessment and one follow up visit. Aside from the prescription medication, the psychiatrist also arranged for a place for me to live. He did not want me living at home and I spent the final six months of high school in foster care.

Eventually, the prescription ran out and I just lived with the tremors. In their day-to-day version, they were manageable. I smoked cigarettes and would light one up if I felt "the shakes" coming on. This pattern set up an emotional addiction to nicotine that lasted long after I no longer smoked daily. I kept cigarettes in the freezer.

about face

What It's Like to Have My Face

Starbucks, at the north end of the first long table, facing the window. On the opposite side, at the south end, a man hunches over his smart phone, thumbs posed on either side, ready to scroll forwards, flip back. He chooses a video—leans in closer, volume low. From time to time, he peeks at me. If I look up, toward the window behind him, he looks. My sight snags his glance, and he looks away. Just now, I look up and my eye is across the street before he raises his head. And so he looks for a long time. Enough time to decide if my face connects us.

And now, he doesn't look at me at all.

Understanding My Face

I had been reading to our five-year-old, my daughter's eyes fixed on the page, her head pressed to my arm, her left hand stroking one of the long vertical creases on the back of the sofa while her toe traced out to the edge of the cushion and back again. My husband was in the bathroom bathing the baby.

I interrupted my reading to answer the phone.

"Guess what," my sister opened. "We're Indians."

We are not a close family, and the distance between my sister and me is both emotional and geographic. We had grown up in Selkirk, Manitoba. Dad worked in the sewers at the steel mill, one of the two major employers in our town, the other being the Selkirk Mental Hospital. Mom ran an informal kindergarten in the basement of the Lutheran Church. My father, too, worked for the church as a janitor. On weekends, he drove taxi. My mother also cooked and did laundry for the grade school teachers and hockey players my parents took in as boarders. Singled out for her striking intelligence and reverent ambitions, my sister had been enticed to leave home to attend a religious boarding school and had gone on to McGill, intending to become a missionary doctor. She had left for school when I was six. We rarely spoke.

My sister plunged into an account of her recent trip all the way from Sacramento, where she had a surgical practice doing *in vitro* fertilizations, to Ste. Anne, a village set on the flat, spirit-levelling grain fields of Manitoba, where our great-grandmother, Euphrosine Curtaz, is buried. My sister is the family genealogist. Her scientific nature means she enjoys research and detail, the task of getting things accurate. She was after a death date and to find it, she needed to find the gravestone. To her, it was a detail worth the distance.

"It was frustrating," she said. "I knew I was in the right place, but I couldn't find her grave."

She said a groundskeeper had noticed her and asked her who she was looking for.

'Caroline Hénault Canada.'

'Oh, you won't find her here,' he told her.

She protested, she said, that she had reliable information our great-great-grandmother was buried in Ste. Anne. I could imagine the nature of this protest. My sister draws a fine line between right and righteous.

'Oh, she's buried in Ste. Anne, all right,' the groundskeeper said. 'But she's not here. You want to find her grave, you're going to have to go to the Indian Reserve.'

This was news.

I hung up the phone. My daughter had left the sofa and joined her sister and my husband in the bathroom. I followed her.

"You'll be surprised by what I just learned," I said. "My great-great-grandmother was an Indian."

My husband was smearing the baby's bottom with a honey-scented beeswax cream that was a keystone in the interlocking of their two lives, its scent the incense of their nightly ritual. He lifted his head from his devotions to look at me, quizzical.

"This is something you just learned?"

My husband was a labour negotiator and had a practiced, measured manner of speaking that he managed to use with warmth. Tall, bearded, wearing out-of-date glasses, and in need of a haircut, he strove to be even-handed more than handsome. At the university where he worked, he was leading a historic battle for pay equity for office workers. He was as likely to take the children to a rally as he was to take them to a folk music festival.

I recounted the call from my sister.

"I don't get it," he said.

I worked on my patience.

"She says I have a great-great-grandmother buried on an Indian Reserve in Manitoba. To be buried on a reserve, you need to a member of a band. A status Indian."

"Yeah, I get that."

"Then what don't you get?"

The five-year-old started adding toys to the cooling bath water.

"I don't get that this is news." He put the night liner in the cotton diaper and slipped it under the baby. "You didn't know you were Aboriginal?"

I tilted my head at him.

"You *did*?"

His voice took on a different tone. Gentler. He, too, was willing to be patient now. Patient and also kind.

"I just always understood you to have Aboriginal heritage. I wondered why you never mentioned it."

The right side of my face tightened and my chin jutted forward. I intensified the question mark I gripped in my expression.

"Remember," he said, "I grew up in Prince Rupert. Dad was a doctor with the federal government. We had people from reserves staying in our home all the time."

This straightened me.

"Staying in your home," I said. I felt I was meeting a part of my husband for the first time, as though a familiar stranger was fastening velcro on my daughter's diaper cover.

"They were waiting to go into the hospital," he explained. "Or they were in town because someone in their family was in the hospital."

My relationship with my husband was not much older than the child he was diapering and I had not met his father. While I knew he worked for the federal government in Prince Rupert, it had not occurred to me that he had been a general practitioner whose practice communities lived on Indian Reserves. Prince Rupert is a port city, and I thought he inspected imports or something. I had very limited understanding of the Canadian constitution. And I had never been to Rupert.

My husband was coaxing the baby into a sleeper. Every once in a while he smiled down at her with the goofy attentiveness he was able to bring this nightly task.

"Why didn't you ever bring it up?" I asked.

"That I understood you were Aboriginal?"

"Exactly."

"I don't know. It just felt unnecessary. Like pointing out your shoe size. I kinda figured I didn't need to mention it."

He picked up the baby, nuzzled her, and handed her to me.

In the bedroom, I opened the lullaby box and let the older girl choose a slip of paper. She pulled out three. We looked at them together, the pencil crayon images and the words. *Ship in a Harbour. Gentle Angry People. Mail Myself to You.* She chose one and I turned down the light. It was a familiar tune. It was what we always did.

The next day, I had tea with my neighbour, Christine. I mentioned the story to her, now struck both by what my sister told me as well as my husband's reaction.

Another blank response. "You didn't know? Wow. It always seemed pretty obvious to me."

Colleagues at work? Same response. I hadn't been passing as white with any of them.

Wake

You dream me still. Racialized, de-racialized, de-colonized. You ask if I have or use a *pre-colonial mind*. You suggest edits to my biography, tell me my stated identity doesn't exist, and that you know this because you are getting a phd in indigenous lit. You ask me flat out if I'm queer, if you can tick off another box on the grant application.

You dream we are friends, and I become someone you get to say you met for tea in the village. You dream we are friends, and you tell me you've taken oranges to the tent city because, of course, that is something I would want to know.

In your dreams, I am often too much, more often not enough. Because of your dreams, you find me repellant, take a prurient interest in my childhood. Your dreams make it hard for me to wake up. I dream I am drowning. I have this dream while I'm awake.

I remember the time we met on the phone, your rude awakening when I showed up at your door. I was still asleep. I checked my shoes to make sure they were clean. As if that had to be the problem.

There was the year you told me it would be best if I chose a different week to rent a cabin, that my daughters were two children too many. You stood beside me on the river bank as I watched the children float by in inner tubes, one of mine vibrant with excitement, the other grinning with fear. I think you dreamed I would never tell.

The grief from that one dreamed me for a long while.

The past is a dream that streams around me, my voice rising through it like bubbles void of vibration, their only sound an almost inaudible pop when they reach the surface. What you cannot see of me fills my lungs.

Always I am waking. I turn up in strange clothes, new words in my mouth, people I no longer know smile as if I remember. I look for others, also awake. Mostly go home alone.

Always I am swimming, cold and asleep, upstream. Bear dips a paw into the stream, flips me breathless against the sky. Wake, he says. Wake.

A Fragile Defiance

You need
only be the simple
expression of the divine
intent
that is your life.
Your breath
an act of insubordination.
To continue breathing is political.
Give voice, seditious.

Be beautiful—subversive.

Every aesthetic has its rules.
Its strategy.

Power.

Your presence the message
think twice.

Smoke

1

It ruined everything,
save the cutlery,
and washable things worth the effort.
The wedding-gift crystal vase? Yes.
But the tent? No.
The cupboard of linens?
Ruined.
Shoes, bath mat,
board games,
umbrellas, plastic ware,
coats.
Books.
Furnishings.
Photographs. Stinks.

You must repurchase your life.

2

Wash, he said, and I bent my face into the smoke,
drew it over my head, brushed my shoulders and each arm.
Down the length of my hair, beneath my raised arms,
his hand swift, sure,
beating the air behind and around me.

3

I bought them in twos and threes,
irritating enough,
but never bummed them.

That welcomed, sharp
first inhalation.

4
This far from the mainland,
the sky is seamless grey,
the sun orange as a harvest moon.
We breathe air off the ocean,
raise prayers.

Winnipeg Trip

My childhood friend posts a photo of us to Facebook and
                        seven of the 19 *likes* it gets
are from women she taught at the Aboriginal training
                        centre in Winnipeg.
It's just a selfie against a flat white sky
taken on a rooftop patio in the Exchange District,
a funky place to stay if you've come halfway across the country
to visit the Métis homeland, and take in the Museum of
                        Human Rights;
and yes, they like her smile and obvious happiness to be
                        with an old friend,
but she knows,
and now I know,
it's my face they're liking.

Who I am is obvious to them.

Although she married a Métis man
and takes her grandchild to the Little Métis nursery school
                        on Thursdays,
lives in Selkirk, for god's sake,
my friend looks at me and doesn't see
Indian.

She sees her friend from school
all grown up and come from far away
but still the same kid
who went to Brownies
skipped double Dutch
and drew a certain amount of awe
by living in a house with an attached garage.

In her mental Rolodex, I don't stand out.
I'm filed under childhood friends
associated with knee socks
and learning to sew on a button.

I was not like the boy who sat in front of me in second grade,
whose shoulders I beat with my ruler every day,
in full sight of my teacher and the kids around me,
until finally he stopped coming to school at all.
I wasn't like him, my friend says.
I didn't smell of woodsmoke.

Commitment

When your second mammogram came back clear, I thought
we'd get a break.
A year ago,
the problem was your husband's drinking the house
into the ground.
You made it through the move to town,
the weeks-old foster child with you.
We talked through strategies to sell the house,
secure divorce,
survive the wrench when the cradled child
left your arms. Months burdened
by your mother's pneumonia,
your father's congestive heart failure.
It was a record-breaking winter.

The point of the trip,
to celebrate.
Like the mammogram,
we were clear.

In Selkirk, I walk the streets,
find our house, the window
of the bedroom where my brother penetrated me
when I was six;
examine the window I leapt from,
age 12, landing barefoot in snow,
my run for blocks in a short-sleeved shirt;

search for the little flat-faced house
where my grandmother sat under an arbour,
cigarettes and a Scrabble board,
the warmth of her palm

as she took my cheek in her hand,
told me I was beautiful,
told me again and again
because she knew
it would get worse
before it got better,
prayed
I would remember.

Away from my own food for seven days,
by the time I get through the two flights,
the train, bus, ferry, car sequence
to my own kitchen,
a night in my own bed,
my gut inflamed,
I shit in my car while driving.

And now this.

My last thoughts at night
are words you said, my friend.
My thoughts on waking,
same.

Two Mornings, 2018

Donald Trump is in a hotel room in Singapore.
We could be hours away from a nuclear war.
I haven't spoken with my friend in Winnipeg for three days.
She isn't speaking to me.

Meanwhile, the sun is high above the house across the street.
The car the neighbour is selling has moved again.
The late iris, abloom in pure purple, its frill and throat on offer.
Drink me.

We make progress.
After five summers of a mud field where we grew peas
        while we waited for inspiration—
five winters of teetering across a makeshift line of concrete
        blocks to get to the front door—
my husband has laid a line of stone the width of our property.
Bones of a wall.

A woman in a coral-coloured sweater stops
                                at the common for a book.
She wears a straw hat.

My friend has elected not to speak.
She fears she will say something empty,
and I will elect
not to be her friend.

I've known her handwriting since the third grade.

. . .

People laugh at me.
As in, *look at those eyeglasses.*

As in, to my face.

This is not the third grade, my eyeglasses not
so thick they distort my eyes.
I am a woman of 58.

Sometimes, they deride me.
Ha. That's just citizenship in the BC Métis.
As if they know my position on race.
Or the Constitution.

My landscaper laughed at my hat.
A boss scoffed at my belt.
A husband laughed at my business plan.

A woman walks down my street in a coral-coloured sweater
and straw hat and I wonder
what else does she get away with?

Boxed

I lack a *fuck off* response

you think I don't see in your eyes
your habit of thought

your arrogance
misogyny
privilege
your manipulative, aggressive nature

I normalize behaviour
reason with abuse

excel on the job, stay in the marriage
suffer meanness

I'd walk away
but I have nowhere I can go

Those I Call Friends

There is in me something immutable.
        Placed there.
                Locatable,
if I breathe just so.

Heaven is the light between the hairs on the borage,
the taste of that blue silk.

Heaven is the memory of women whose necks
        have taken my cheek, whose
                ribs have risen
    beneath my arms.
Women who slake a thirst in me.
        By talent or a bright edge.
                By a look direct to my eye.
Women whose wit, or willingness,
        feeds me still.

They are here. Along with the drill of hummingbirds,
        despite the ragged caw of crows.
                What has been unwound
lies loose;
        what has been joined,
                knits still.

And they are absent. Sting on the instinct to long for that nectar.

To be washed of this longing
     for the imaginative,
          for the magnetic.
To become a woman who eats plum cake, drinks tea.
     Arrives clean, armed with rhubarb. Heart dry
          from the long, low burn of loyalty.

Duck Ugly

In a corner of the attic, my husband has found
the long-lost box of photographs. To quell my ache,
I have been seeing them as ashes.

My eyes feel hungry.
I wait days.

Select a set of my face looking straight at the camera,
hold them close.
Long.

The over-exposed photo of my last night primigravida,
my feet in a bowl of water and petals,
my midwife seated on the floor,
is not over-exposed. She is merely very white
beside me.

I am the brown child at the birthday party.
I am the brown child in the Grade 4 picture.

It is not shadow. It is not always summer.

This round-faced girl with the winsome smile,
slender and graceful young woman,
again and again I find her
as I search for an image to show me how I looked
back in the days I was ugly.

Beneficiaries of a Genocide

| After listening to "Beneficiary" by Wintersleep,
and reading Peter Carey interviewed in The Guardian,
November 18, 2017.

You. Who cannot call yourself settler.
That's
what I want you to call yourselves.

You. Who speak about me in the third person, even though
I've introduced myself
and am sitting right here.

Who say stupid things without knowing it.

Like: *But don't you sometimes wish you had a status card?*
And: *I don't see why they don't do better by themselves; I mean,*
                         they get a free education.

I don't care if you came here only 60 years ago,
or how bad your ancestors had it in the place you came from,
or you think the real problem is capitalism.
Or any other reason you *don't identify with colonialism.*
You're still settlers, all of you.
If your family came into the country under the authority
    of an asserted power calling itself the Government of Canada,
you are, in the terminology of that self-same entity

                                still in use today,
a settler.

It pains me to explain your government to you.

I don't imagine you'll like this term any better.
Beneficiary of a genocide.
But I think it narrows the argument.

How much longer do we have to hear about your very real pain
before you will have a conversation with us about ours?

How much longer will you ask that your immediate needs
take precedence over the fundamentals of our existence?

What does it mean, this Aboriginal title? Does it mean they
            own the land? Are they going to come and take it back?

Yes. And, as a matter of fact...

But put that aside. I will leave the future
to explain itself to you. For now
let us stay in the present.

Let us stay in this room where you are now uncomfortable
and I am now unwelcome.

Let us begin with what you call yourselves.

Slow

I am not required to travel fast,
much as desire might draw.
What happened then is still not past.

I don't know the role I'm cast,
the shape and nature of my flaw.
I am not required to travel fast.

I answer, even come when asked;
wait for the cold to thaw.
What happened then is still not past.

My spirit bruised, my heart harassed,
the long-rubbed spot still raw.
I am not required to travel fast.

If it's true, you've drunk your last,
set right a years-long yaw,
what happened then is still not past.

I could, with time I will perhaps
spin beauty out of straw;
for now, I will not travel fast.
What happened then is still not past.

Sometimes You Learn Things Quite Late in the Game
| *after the Russian fairy tale "Vasilisa the Beautiful."*

Hit them with a wooden spoon when they're small;
when they are older, you will only need to raise it.

We all do it. Face Baba Yaga. Find ourselves
                     without a mother in a dark wood.

We pass by the skulls on the fence as if children,
unafraid. Enter the door of a hut dancing on chicken legs as if
this was a place to find shelter. Find ourselves confronted by
an old woman
and a stove.

Don't think we don't see the danger.
We walk through her gate and enter her door open-faced,
every time.

Hoofbeats on air,
the latch on the curse clicks shut.

Grain by grain, look for fly shit.
The speck of impending death.

In time, you learn.

You trust the voice in your pocket.

And hands appear.
Baba Yaga whirls through the sky
and you are unafraid.
Not because you are brave.
Because you are free.

No matter how often one enters the hut,
the way out is always the same.

Something Purple

By the first day of pow wow
I'd been on the land three days.
Time enough to find my way around the arbour.
Time enough to make a friend or two.
Time enough to settle into drum beats.
Time to become a face
in the stands.

Day two, I am offered tobacco.
Will I pray?
I take up the tobacco, wait for the Red Dress Special.
Pray for the families wrenched by sorrow.
Pray for the women whose fates
sicken.
Pray for healing.
Pray men join us.
Return to my seat, arms
filled with gifts.

It rains the last day,
the pow wow moves indoors.
Fancy-dance bustles hang between panes of arena glass,
eagle feather fans, beaded shields.
Mothers discipline long brown locks into braids,
lace brilliant breastplates into place,
clip barrettes, tie chokers, add earrings.

I buy a bag of saskatoon berries from a couple with a cooler,
lunch on berry laden fry bread,
search the stands for the people I know,
gift them with salmon I brought for saying
mwêstas. see you later.

A woman I met before the dancing
approaches me, stops my breath with shine and sparkle,
her regalia magnifying her, magnificent.
She offers to present me to the Chief.
His headdress humbles me,
stumbles my tongue.
He says I am welcome to return,
seals the invitation with a blanket,
purple and tan, an orange stripe,
black trim.

"Untitled," by Markus Drassl, from the series Rendering Intent, 2020. Ink on paper, 60" × 48".

what it is like to be this extreme and appear normal

| after "Untitled" (from the series Rendering Intent) by Markus Drassl

1

I needed to learn   to inhabit my face

     slow my heart with my gaze

     stand my ground in the space you create
     when you look at me
       step away from the recoil
       in an otherwise civil face
         (the eye does not lie)

2

when practicing vowels in a new language
let your cheeks hang from your face
your jaw unhinge from your ear
balance your head over your esophagus

the *i* of my name, the echolocation
that finds me

3

there's a trick I do with my foot, the way I rock
get my knee over my ankle
when blood pounds in my eye
keep my balance

4

a woman wearing these clothes is

                who?

5

the diaphragm drops
the pelvis settles
the gut roils

6

there is a way to breathe

       if you want not to be heard
       if your cloud of breath is life leaving you
       if your heart is a fire hall bell
       when you're shot in midair
       when words silence thought
       if you want to remember
       if your next move

                          is to leap

7

it's a tough starting point
weed seed on dry ground

The Other Grandmother

There were times I would sense the contours of my face
(perhaps I was tired)
(perhaps relaxed)
—would try to hold my features perfectly still, walk
gently to a mirror to catch
a glimpse of what I looked like
in that state.

Check if with that expression,
I looked like my grandmother.
Her long face.
Her flamboyant indifference.
Her mannishness.
Her brazen disregard for good taste
in mixed company.

Check—was I ugly?

There were times I tried to memorize
the feeling of enough of a smile to
lift the sag of my cheek, dull line
of my mouth.

Brighten my brow
with an arch.

Tried to recreate the image
I would sometimes see
—walking alongside the glass wall of the bank, or
coming out of a toilet stall—
a woman I didn't recognize,

breathtakingly thin
in a navy Ports suit.

She'd show up in photos
the bullrush on the arm of a chair,
white turtleneck cable knit sheath—
an arc of laughter.

Who was she?

Then yesterday,
seated across from a mirror
—a happenstance long look.
The stranger
surfaced.
Stayed.

We had come to terms,
my face
and I.

The grandmother
I no longer sculpted away,

and this one.

Self-Portrait of the Poet

She reclines in bed, in a room
                              the colour of red earth,
          against a silk pillow
                    the colour of straw late on a September afternoon.
               She is dressed in a black sweater,
          her long hair a companion down her left side.

Over her right shoulder,
                              we see out a window.
Hawthorns,   berries garnet,   leaves still lush
          against the lit white sky.

Her eyebrows are precise, dark
                              arches, her ears larger
          than previous self-portraits.

The light silvers her steel grey hair,
                    brightens her skin (pores
                                        visible).
Head slightly right,
               the skin of her neck drapes.
          Her lip and chin, nude of bristle.

The eye of the self-portrait, the eye of one
unafraid to look.   What is to be found
in this examination? We know nothing
from a face.   On what curve of cheek
does the world see *wife of an alcoholic*?
What detail points at *tinnitus*?

Features, her features, are silent.
The portrait says only one thing:
go ahead. look.
Look as long as you like.

addendum

Victoria, British Columbia

Dear Mother,

I am writing to explain my absence as I am finally able to articulate it.

It is, perhaps, mysterious to you that I have not contacted you since the weekend you spent with us in May, 2010. Shortly after your visit, I became ill. I have not worked since then and have, in fact, been forced into medical retirement due to mental illness.

I'd like you to know I received your phone message on my birthday. I want also to respond to your request that we renew family relations.

I regret, this request is not one I can meet.

In our interactions, you have insisted, and continue to insist, that we leave "the past in the past."

This is not an option for me. Because of events in my childhood relating to my brother, Stephen, I suffer from Post Traumatic Stress Disorder and associated depression and anxiety. My condition is severe enough that it has now cost me my career.

I live with the consequences of childhood sexual abuse and violence every day. Medical retirement is allowing me to slowly recover from the bout of severe depression that drove me from work and is only now receded to a level that I can function moderately. For a time, in 2010 and 2011, I was unable to manage even basic daily functions like bathing or dressing or preparing simple meals. Without the loving care of my husband, my quality of life would have been grim.

In order to maintain my gains in recovery, I must exercise great caution not to over extend myself. I have regained sufficient cognitive capacity that I can now do my own banking, do some volunteer work, and write. I am, however, restricted in the number of people with whom I have regular contact, needing to be on constant guard against individuals who display any signs of aggressive tendencies, including passive-aggressive stress coping behaviour. There are few people in my world.

It is essential to my mental health that I spend considerable time in creative process.

I think daily about what happened to me in childhood, either because of waking from a nightmare, because of the drive to write, because I am preparing to participate in a community event on mental health—or because I have slept in my clothes for the second night in a row following a social encounter that broke through my very fragile social defences.

I intend to speak publicly about my life. I have changed my name to Brown and have gone under that name for some years now. There is no need for people who know you, but do not know me, to associate my life with you. That is, you can continue to keep the secret.

But I can't.

What you need to know, however, is that, in fact, you are making a choice. The reason I cannot see you is that I cannot be in the same room as the secret. To even imagine being in the same room as the secret takes my breath away. My throat has closed. My heart is pounding.

Thus, if you wish to spend time with me, you will need to deal with the secret. Talk about it with me and admit it to others.

You can't keep the secret and have me, too. Because I can't do it any more. It's over.

I will be 56 years old next April. Next year is the 50th anniversary of the beginning. Fifty years is long enough.

Your daughter,
Michelle

poetic statement

I write as a refusal to be silenced.

I write to resist shame.

I write as an answer to questions I'm tired of explaining.

I write to put down my side of the story.

I write because my manner of speaking is so slow.

I write in response to the narrative that knocks incessantly.

I write to put things down so I can move on.

I write, also, to amuse myself. I like the way words feel in my mouth and the way they sound in my head. I enjoy observation. At those times, it feels like play.

| We are, each of us, walking-around, knowing beings, holding ideas and memories that show in our gait, in the way we hold our face. A poem is an exercise in bringing forward from the body the sense of a moment—following my breath, the rise of my spine, the sense of my skin as I sit on a rock watching a heron hunt, or in my garden listening to bees in the borage, or as I walk an urban street and smell toast.

Even event poems—today in my marriage, this; that day when sun poured into the veranda—are coloured by how I balance on my legs, what I am digesting. An event lingers as an ache, nudges in a turning of my head.

Whether I begin in nature, in the shine of light on the leaves of our plum tree, or in form, the skeleton and nails of a given rhythm and rhyme scheme, it is the sense at the back of my throat that I am trying to articulate. To see if you, too, can feel the constriction there, if you, too, will take a beat and say *yes*, or smile wryly halfway down the page. The tiny gesture, even one entirely unnoticed (the momentary drop in blood pressure that can accompany recognition)—that is what I'm after. An effect on the breath is a prize.

acknowledgements

My husband, Stephen Brown. My treasured first reader. For the ever reassuring invitation, *When you feel comfortable, I would like to hear it.* And the gentle, insightful response that always makes it better.

My cultural advisor, Bernadette Spence, for her wisdom and her medicine and her love.

maskwamitêh Lila Ferguson.   Emma Pickering.

Chelsea Comeau, who is the best friend a poem could have—and who has become, in the process, my friend, too. For her vision. And her standards.

My coach and confidante, Deb Williams, whose light has been inspiring me for years and years.

My mentor and guide, Betsy Warland. Who made possible the poet who wrote this book.

The people who created and those who continue to sustain the Sage Hill Writing program. May every one of you be blessed. Sandra Ridley, who taught me the move from the diving board.

The First Peoples' Cultural Council, BC, for awarding me an Artist Grant in 2019 to undertake a 67-day poetic inquiry in a 1987 Dodge B250 Caravan, covering territory from Ile de Chênes to Palmbere Lake to Maskwacis.

All the people who took me in, treated me as family.

Some of these poems have been previously published, or otherwise recognized, sometimes in slightly different form:

"5:53 PM" and "Slow" were published in "The Length of a Day", a song cycle for tenor and piano (Jeffrey Ryan, composer). Commissioned by Pacific Opera Victoria for Colin Ainsworth, it received its World Premiere via online stream from the Baumann Centre in Victoria, British Columbia, Canada, on April 16, 2021.

"Beneficiaries of a Genocide" and "A Perspective on Women" were published in *Arc Poetry Magazine 92*, "Response to Missing and Murdered Women" issue, in 2020. "A Perspective on Women" was also published for the League of Canadian Poets' Poetry Pause in February 2021.

"Duck Ugly" was published in *Emrys Journal* in 2021, and was shortlisted for the Federation of BC Writers Literary Writes Contest in 2020.

"A Fragile Defiance" was published in *Literary Review of Canada* in March 2022.

"The Girls I Grew Up With Are Everywhere" received an Honourable Mention for the *This Magazine* National Poetry Competition in 1990.

"The House on Strathnaver Avenue" was published in *The Fieldstone Review* in 2017.

"Lasts" was published in *Grain Magazine 46.5* "Indigenous Writers & Storytellers" issue in 2019.

"Those I Call Friends" was published in *Grain Magazine 47.2* "Of Auburn And Blue" issue in 2020.

"Two Mornings, 2018" (as "Porch Poems") and "Winnipeg Trip" were published in the chapbook *i am what becomes of broken branch: A Collection of Voices by Indigenous Poets in Canada*, released by the League of Canadian Poets and the Saskatchewan Aboriginal Writers Circle in 2020. "Porch Poems" was long listed for the *Room Magazine* Poetry Contest 2019.

"Smoke" was published in *Fresh Voices: Tending the Fire,* part of the chapbook series released by the League of Canadian Poets in 2020.

"Understanding My Face" is an excerpt from a piece by the same name, forthcoming from Demeter Press in the anthology *Don't Tell: Family Secrets* in 2023, and was shortlisted for *Event Magazine's* Nonfiction Contest in February 2020.

"Under the Covers" was published in *The Sun Magazine's* Readers Write column in November 1996.

"Wake" was published in *PRISM international 57.1* "Dreams" issue in 2018, and in the Festival of Literary Diversity in April 2020. It was nominated for the Pushcart Prize and awarded the Earle Birney Prize for Poetry, 2019.

"Walk on the Left-Hand Side" was published in *CV2 Magazine 42.1* "Summer" issue in 2019.

"what it is like to be this extreme and appear normal" was published in the chapbook *ekphrasis: poets respond to arc-hive studio artists* published by Arc-Hive Studio in 2020.

The Bad Wife

MICHELINE MAYLOR

Micheline Maylor's *The Bad Wife* is an intimate, first-hand account of how to ruin a marriage. This poetry collection is a story of divorce, love, and what should have been, told in a brave and unflinching voice.

Robert Kroetsch Series

Gospel Drunk

AIDAN CHAFE

Aidan Chafe's *Gospel Drunk* is a personal journey to find clarity and identity in the face of alcoholism and religion. Sharp, intoxicating imagery and a gutsy, minimalist aesthetic combine in these poems to explore some of our darkest and strongest belief systems, dismantling them with wit and wisdom.

Robert Kroetsch Series

I Am Still Your Negro

An Homage to James Baldwin

VALERIE MASON-JOHN

Spoken-word poet Valerie Mason-John unsettles readers with potent images of ongoing trauma from slavery and colonization. *I Am Still Your Negro* is truth that needs to be told, re-told, and remembered.

Robert Kroetsch Series

More information at uap.ualberta.ca